BEING ON THE PLANET

1 A DIARY OF TRUE EVENTS

By

Jaclyn (Clark) Hodge

ISBN 978 1-7335817-5-2
Manufactured in the United States of America

BEING ON
THE PLANET
1
A DIARY OF TRUE EVENTS
NEW
BOOK COVER
BEING ON
THE PLANET
Jaclyn Clark Hodge

BEING ON THE PLANET 1

A DIARY OF TRUE EVENTS

TABLE OF CONTENTS

Acknowledgements

To my mother Rose X (Clark) Morris, I give a special thank you. I couldn't have finished this work if it wasn't for her. Mom is the publisher and co-editor of this book. She is also the Author and Publisher of the book, Chronicle of the Seventh Son, Black Panther Mark Clark. It's been an honor and a pleasure to work with her again on another book. To my mother and my stepfather Brian Morris, I thank you and I love you both!

To my immediate family; Perry, Perry Jr., Paris, Peru, and Porsche. I dedicate this book to you all. You are the heartbeat of my life! I thank you all and I love you all forever!

To my nephew Isaiah (Alexander) Hodge. While I was writing, you always wanted to read my stories. You were always interested in each and every memory I shared with you. Isaiah, you kept me motivated to complete the book. Thank you, auntie loves you! Also, to my cousin Cassanova Bowers for his listening ear and inspiration; thank you, I love you cousin!

To my dad Phil Hodge Sr. and his wife (Sherry), and to my brothers Phil, Marcus, Aaron, and Caleb. I thank you and I love you all!

In memory of my beloved Grandparents, Roy and Katherine Hodge and Elder William and Missionary Fannie Mae Clark. I am very grateful for the sacrifices you made, the life you lived, and the legacy you have passed on. Thank you. I love you all!

To each and every one of my family members that I didn't get to mention, I love you all!

Forward

Being On The Planet, A Diary of True Events is a page turner and a must read gripping story. The author, Jaclyn (Clark) Hodge shares memories that have happened throughout her life. Some of her memories are about real-life UFO encounters. In vivid detail, the author describes the UFO encounters and she tells about how her family were affected afterwards. She provides information from in depth conversations that she has had with her mother, Rose X (Clark) Morris, a witness who has experienced mental telepathy with the Mother Wheel. She also shares a conversation with her brother Phil (Jr.) about a foreign implant found in his body after a UFO encounter, and she explains his response. In this book, the Author shares several UFO encounters that she has had over a period of years.

Introduction

First of all, I want to give you a big welcome into my world. Welcome! My name is Jaclyn (Clark) Hodge and I am the author and co-editor of this memoir. I am also a person who believes in UFOs. I know they exist because I have witnessed them more than a couple of times throughout my life. In this book, I tell pieces of my life story and share memories of the UFO encounters and other weird phenomena that happened to my family. I describe the five different sightings that occurred during my childhood, early adulthood, and after I started a family of my own. I also include my special memories such as giving birth to my children. Although this book is a little out of the norm, it's all true. I want everyone who reads my book to know that I am not a UFO expert and I'm not trying to convince anyone into believing in UFOs or aliens. I'm just simply telling my account of what happened.

The summer of 1984 was when my family had our first UFO encounter. At that time, I was only seven years old. My younger brother (Phil Jr.) was just six. My brother (Marcus) was a five month old baby. My other brothers (Aaron and Caleb) hadn't been born yet. My dad (Phil Sr.) and my mom (Rose) were a married couple back then, both in their mid-twenties. We were a young and vibrant family traveling down the highway in a brand new Buick LeSabre. Suddenly, a great giant ball of fire appeared in the sky. It seemed to be moving in the same direction as our vehicle traveled on the highway. The very thought of the ball of fire falling was upsetting to my dad. As dad sped down the highway trying to outrun it, the huge ball of fire quickly passed us by. About fifteen minutes later, a massive UFO appeared. It was about a half mile long and it flew right above our vehicle. During the experience, my mother said that she had mental telepathy with the UFO. After the encounter, my parents noticed that a weird electrical anomaly had occurred which caused the clock in the brand new car to stop working. My story begins in Flint, Michigan on July 23, 1984.

BEING ON THE PLANET

1 A DIARY OF TRUE EVENTS

Chapter One

Our Vacation Was a "Trip"

(1984)

Memories 1-10

Memory 1 - Preparing For The Road

It was July 23, 1984. At approximately 11 am, I was sitting on the porch waiting to leave for our vacation. My parents were still in the house getting prepared. While I waited, I looked over at my dad's brand new, all white, four door, Buick LeSabre and I mapped out where everyone would sit. I knew that my dad would definitely be the official driver and my mom would ride on the passenger side. In the back seat, right in the middle; there was a baby car seat and my brother Marcus would sit there. There were only two seats left. So, I contemplated beating my other younger brother Phil Jr. to the seat that I wanted.

About five minutes later, mom and dad walked out of the front door and passed by. Mom was carrying my baby brother and she had snacks for our trip. Dad was putting the luggage in the trunk. Then mom said, "Jaclyn and Phil Jr. get in the car!" After hearing that, I became so excited. Phil Jr. and I quickly raced to the car and we claimed our seats. I sat on the left side and he sat on the right just as I had planned.

While we were waiting in the car, my dad did his house check. He was unable to leave the house until he double and triple checked if the stove was off. After coming back and forth to the car and then leaving again, mom said, "Hey Phil, it's okay, come on let's go!" It seemed like dad was taking forever. After about twenty minutes, he finally sat in the vehicle. As he strapped on his seatbelt, mom smiled and happily spoke, "Is everybody ready to ride?" With excitement, Phil Jr. and I both responded with "yeah" from the backseat. Then dad reached his hand towards the radio and he put his Isley Brothers music into the deck. It would be the soundtrack of our adventure. As we pulled out of the driveway, the song *Voyage to Atlantis* started blasting through the speakers. For the next thousand miles, it would be replayed over and over again.

Around 11:30 am, we finally left from our home on Marlowe Drive in Flint, Michigan and we headed out to our destination. We were going to the beautiful State known for its unique Creole and Cajun culture, jazz music, and Mardi Gras festivals. New Orleans, Louisiana was also the location of the 1984 World's Fair which mom wanted us to attend. She especially wanted us to see NASA's first space shuttle, the Enterprise which was on display. We couldn't wait to get to Louisiana.

Memory 2 - Looking Out Of The Window

Once we hit the highway, I looked out of the left side backseat window and I watched the scenery. We were rolling fast and as we quickly passed by; I paid special attention to the yellow highway strips in the road for hours. I also took notice of the electrical power lines which were so tall in the air. Around dusk, the Isley Brothers music was still playing. By then, the guitar riff and the lyrics ``I'll Always Come Back To You" were forever etched in my mind. Eventually, I couldn't keep my eyes open and I fell asleep. I don't know how long I slept but for a brief moment I did wake up in the middle of the night. The last thing that I can remember is my family being on a pitch black highway. I looked up into the front seat and I noticed that the music had stopped playing and my parents were driving in total silence. Through the front window, I saw the car's hood glowing bright white. After noticing that, I was so tired; I fell right back to sleep.

Memory 3 - When I Awoke

July 24, 1984 around 7am, I awoke in the backseat of the car and my little brothers were still asleep. The morning air came through the window and the sun started to beam into the car. On a beautiful summer morning, we were parked at a McDonalds restaurant. The restaurant had well cut green grass and clean pavement. It looked so much different from some of the McDonalds in Flint. I had a sense that I was somewhere prominent and I felt good and refreshed.

I asked my parents, "where are we at"; but mom and dad paid no attention to me. As I listened to them, it seemed as if they were whispering and mumbling in the front seat. I really wanted to ask for some McDonalds but I decided not to bother them while they were talking. I figured that they must be in a serious conversation and I automatically knew not to interrupt. As I continued to listen, my parents were saying words like, UFO and spaceship and ball of fire. I didn't really know what a spaceship was. I thought that they only existed in cartoons. Then, as if I was an adult who understood the subject; mom hysterically started to inform me on what occurred.

Memory 4 - The Ball Of Fire and UFO

My mother told me that while we were driving down the highway, a huge flaming ball of fire appeared above the road. She said that it happened somewhere in Missouri. Then mom said, "Sometime around dusk, the ball of fire started traveling along with our car and it seemed as if it was following us from the sky." Mom stated that my dad said, "Rose, If that ball of fire falls, it will blow us all up!" Immediately, he punched the gas. Mom said that dad generated the car to about 90 miles per hour trying to out-run the ball of fire on the highway. Then mom said that the ball of fire rapidly passed us until it was soon out of sight. After the ball of fire zoomed past us, we continued driving down the highway. Fifteen minutes later, it went from dusk to darkness outside.

As darkness came, mom looked out of the passenger window and she noticed a great giant lit-up mother ship in the night sky. She thought it was about a half a mile by a half a mile. Mom said, "It was so gigantic, it should have been seen coming but it just instantly appeared out of nowhere!" Then she said that she told my dad, "that looks like a spaceship Phil" and she said that my dad said, "yeah it does look like a spaceship." Then mom said that the UFO moved over the top of the vehicle encompassing the entire sky.

As the UFO covered our car, mom experienced mental telepathy. Her thoughts were on what she calls a "loudspeaker". Mom mentally asked, "Are you God?" She heard the reply, "God Is A Word That Man Created." She also heard, "We Are Brothers In A Coalition For Universal Peace." Mom said that the great vehicle began to give her even more answers. It told her that one day something was going to happen to the planet and they are going to help some of the people. Suddenly, mom noticed that dad was crying out saying, "Jesus help us, please don't hurt us!"

Mom said that my dad had been hysterically crying out for a while but she was sort of zoned out and didn't notice him at first. Once mom did notice that dad was in distress, she started to get afraid. She said that she wasn't even scared of the UFO until dad's cries made her afraid. Then mom said," Lord please withdraw yourself from us, please go away!" Mom said that after she asked it to go away, she could feel the UFO leaving but she never actually watched it leave. Then mom said, "we continued driving down the highway but we were all in some sort of daze-like state." She said that it was as if everything in the car (including us) wasn't working correctly. The clock in the new car mysteriously stopped working. It was affected by some sort of weird electrical anomaly that occurred during the encounter.

Memory 5 - I Better Not Tell

After mom told me that a spaceship was right above our car on the highway, dad complained about how the clock had stopped working in the brand new car. Then mom said, "Jaclyn, they spoke to my mind!" I wondered who "they" actually were but I was too afraid to ask. I didn't quite understand the conversation that mom was having with me but it was interesting. After listening, I became a bit disappointed that I had slept through the whole thing and I wished that I was awake when they saw the UFO. Suddenly, with anger; dad said, "Don't you tell anybody what happened to us when we get to Louisiana or they will think that we're crazy!" In fear of getting a whooping, I said, "okay, I won't tell nobody." I knew by his demeanor that he meant business. By the look in my parents eyes, I could tell that they were not playing around.

Although the concept of a UFO was beyond my intellect, the one thing that I did surely know was that my dad was subjected to whoop me if I disobeyed him. I was more afraid of my dad's belt than anything else in the whole world. So, I didn’t plan on telling anyone. After dad made it very clear that we shouldn’t tell his family in Louisiana about the UFO, everyone in the car became quiet.

Memory 6 - We Arrived In Louisiana

As we drove through Louisiana, the weather was hot. It was so hot until my behind was burning from the car's sun baking seats. While I squirmed around to get relief, Phil Jr. spoke and awkwardly said, "My booty is melting." My mother and I just cracked up laughing, it was funny and the way he said it was so cute! I was sweating profusely too so I knew what he meant. It felt like we were in the desert. Actually, for the first time; I saw a giant heatwave at the intersection. It was flaring down the street moving in an array of many colors. I kept thinking, "It's so dang-on hot, a heat wave is walking down the street." I hadn't ever seen anything like it before in Flint, Michigan. In the extreme heat, we drove along until we came upon this dirt road with a long picket fence. It seemed as if we drove down that dirt road for miles and I became very anxious to get to our destination.

Memory 7 - My Great Grandparents Farm

[redacted]

Finally, we arrived at my great grandparents Standard and Mildred Stevens' farm. We were in Plain Dealing, Louisiana. I leaped out of the car, stretched, and looked out into the acres and acres of land. I heard crickets and snakes and all kinds of other noises coming from the environment. I noticed that there were horses and cows and chickens and hogs too. I even read a sign that said, "beware of the alligators" and I became afraid.

When I saw that my parents were being greeted by family members, I thought about how mom and dad saw the UFO. As soon as that thought entered my mind, I remembered that I shouldn't tell any of my dad's family members about it. I knew that it was a secret that I should keep because I might get a whooping if I didn't. So, I just went to explore the farm.

First, I stopped by the barn. When I looked inside, I saw about forty hogs. I felt comfortable watching them as they oinked around and it felt like they didn't mind me watching. Suddenly, my great granddad came over to the shed that was right next to the barn and he grabbed his shotgun. When the hogs heard him cock his gun, they all immediately started to cry and squeal. I couldn't believe that the hogs were intelligent enough to know that he was getting a gun. They didn't even see him but they heard him. Before great granddad could walk over to me, the hogs were all running and pushing to the back of the barn. It looked as if they were trying to cover each other up in a huddle. Even the tiny ones knew that they better get in the huddle too. Then, my great granddad stood right next to me. I looked up at him and said, "The pigs are crying!" He said, "Girl that's food, get out of the way!" My great granddad pointed in the hogs direction and I covered my ears as he shot his gun. After the blast, he walked into the barn and he dragged one of the medium sized hogs out. All of the other hogs whimpered about the loss of their loved one and I was really sad for them and their situation.

Later on that day, Phil Jr. went exploring inside of the chicken coupe. He must have bothered their eggs because he suddenly ran out screaming. I saw about thirty chickens swooping on top of him. I watched as he fell on the ground and was mobbed with multiple pecks. As I called for help, my great granddad came and said to the chickens, "Get off that boy and go back into the coupe." They suddenly stopped pecking my brother and all strutted into the coupe as they were told. From that day on, I realized that farm animals are quite intelligent.

Unfortunately, for those animals; as the day went on; that hog that my great-grandfather had shot and some of those chickens that pecked my brother was sliced down the middle and slowly barbecued in a pit in the ground. Although I was sad for the animals' death, they were smoked to perfection and I admit, they were delicious.

Memory 8 - The 1984 World's Fair

July 25, 1984. It was my mom's birthday. That morning, we had big slabs of bacon and eggs fresh off the farm. Although mom does not eat pork anymore, at the time it was the best breakfast that we've ever tasted! After spending the night at the farm, we were headed to The 1984 World's Fair and Exhibition in New Orleans, Louisiana. We didn't know it at the time but it would be the last World's Fair in the United States.

While we drove there, I was looking over the Mississippi River and wondering how much longer would it be until we arrived. When we got there, we took a memorable family photo in front of the entrance. After entering the exhibition, there was this giant statue of the Greek God Neptune. He had a trident in his hand while he stood above this majestic lady with gators all around her. My family took a picture in front of that statue as well. I vaguely remember the amusement rides but I do remember one of them though. It had a sun's face on it and it spun round and round. Last but not least, I remember seeing the Nasa Space Shuttle exhibit. It was called The Enterprise. After all of the fun and excitement, I slept the whole way back to Flint, Michigan. I don't remember anything about the drive back home.

Memory 9 - In the Backyard

Sometime after we returned from our vacation, Phil Jr. and I were playing in the backyard of our house on Marlowe Drive in Flint, Michigan. It was on a sunny day. I was playing basketball with a hoop made out of a crate. It was nailed to our old tree. Suddenly, I noticed that my brother was near the garage slouched down as if something was wrong with him. When I came closer, I saw him picking at a cut on his right knee. My brother was always picking at his scars and being a big sister, it seemed as if I was always asking for him to let me see. We would usually just wrap up a cut and go on with our day but not this time.

When Phil Jr. allowed me to look at his new gash, it wasn't normal so I couldn't just put a bandage on it. Oddly, there was this thin black object sticking about one inch out of the right side of his right knee and pus was all around it. I thought, "how in the world did that thing get in there?" At first, I thought it was some type of stinger in his knee but it wasn't. I asked my brother, "do it hurt" and he said, "no". Being as careful as I could, I started to slowly tweeze at the object with my fingers. As I pulled, his knee should have bled but there was no blood at all; only pus came out of the joint.

As I continued to pull, I became extremely worried. The length of the weird object was much longer than I anticipated.

When the object was protruding out of Phil Jr's. knee about seven more inches, I couldn't believe that it hadn't come out yet. Eventually, within a few more minutes of pulling and gently wiggling; it finally came all the way out. The whole object was about ten to twelve inches long; which was about the length from his knee down to his foot. In shock of what just happened, I asked Phil Jr., "are you ok" and he said, "yeah”. Then I held the strange long rod up to my eyes and I got a really good look at it.

Memory 10 - The Weird Long Object

The weird long object that I pulled out of my brother's knee was about ten to twelve inches long. It was similar to a wire hanger from the closet or an antenna on the car but it was as thin as a medium size sewing needle. The end of it wasn't pointy though. It was rounded off. Although it looked like black metal, the material of the weird object was actually more like a rock. It was like a blackish long granite stone or a blackish long piece of lead but it looked like metal. The weird object was flimsy and sort of flexible too.

As I stood by the garage, I put the weird object up into the sunlight. That's when I noticed that it had some very tiny writings and symbols embedded on it as well. The small etchings resembled the Medu Neter on the Egyptian Pyramids. At that time, we were just small children and we didn't know anything about hieroglyphics. The experience was so bazaar until my seven year old mind couldn't process it correctly. I didn't know what the heck it was and I couldn't figure it out. In total confusion, I threw the weird object on the ground in the backyard of our house. Then the both of us kept playing like nothing ever happened. We didn't even tell our parents and I don't know why. Maybe we didn't tell our parents because we were tough children who didn't cry to our parents about cuts and bruises. Or, maybe we just had short attention spans at those ages. I don't know what was the reason but it was as if we just instantly forgot all about it. It would be seven years later when we would finally speak about the weird long object.

BEING ON THE PLANET 1
A DIARY OF TRUE EVENTS

Chapter Two

Time To Remember

(1991)

Memories 11-15

Memory 11 - The Broken Family

In the summer of 1991, my family was going through turmoil. My mom and dad had broken up and my younger brothers (Phil Jr., Marcus, and Aaron) and myself had our lives flipped upside down. I was a fourteen year old teenager who suffered from anxiety and depression because of my parents drama. Also, I didn't get along with mom's new boyfriend and mom wanted me to accept the major life transition which was too hard for me to cope with. I was very unhappy and it seemed as if I was living two different lives.

In one portion of life, I remembered that I had good parents, a close family, a great best friend, I grew up in a decent neighborhood, I was a church kid, a band musician, a poet, and a basketball player for various teams. On the other prospective; I became somewhat of a rebel who experimented with smoking cigarettes, weed, alcohol, and sex to deal with the emotional pain. I wasn't being continuously monitored or secluded from those things that had a negative effect on me. I concealed some of it from my family but some of my behavior was accepted because I was seen as such a well mannered mature teenager who everyone treated like an adult.

When my mom found out about my depression, she sent me to counseling but I ran away from the counseling facility. It resulted in me being simply ignored. At fourteen years of age, I moved in with my older cousin (Melissa). I lived as if I was an adult and I never moved back home.

Memory 12 - The Clock In Dad's Car

One day, in the summer of 1991; my dad picked me up from my grandmother's house. He wanted to talk to me about my mom and he was checking up on my little brothers. At the time, the youngest boys were staying with my grandmother (Fannie Mae Clark). She's my mother's mother. Being the oldest child, I did realize when my dad picked me up that he and my mom were about to finalize their divorce. I was sad about their breakup but the music in the old Buick made me feel better.

As I rode with dad in the old LeSabre, the song *Everlasting Love* by Tony Terry came on the radio. It was such a beautiful love song and it was the first time that I heard it. While the music played, my dad drove me to the store. After listening to that masterpiece, dad went into the store and he picked out the snacks for me and he got himself a drink. When he returned to the car, he drove straight to the house on Marlowe Drive. It was the house where I grew up and where we lived as a family before my mom and dad started having relationship problems. While blasting the radio, we parked in the driveway. Once my dad turned the music down, we started having our father daughter talk. We were only talking for about five minutes when suddenly the clock in the car caught our attention. The gauge on the minute hand just flipped over and started working again as if it was never broken.

The clock hadn't worked at all since our UFO encounter in 1984. The way it clicked back on was odd! My dad and I were both a bit stunned. It was even kind of creepy.In shock, we just looked at each other with a serious gaze. It was so weird that seven years later the clock would just pop on like that. It instantly caused me to remember what happened back in 1984. Although I slept through the UFO experience, I did have a memory of my own that I hadn't even told anyone. I remembered the weird object that I pulled out of my brother's knee. I wanted to talk to my dad about what I remembered but I was too afraid to tell him.

Memory 13 - The Talk With Bro

I spoke with Phil Jr. and I told him about how the clock in dad's car was now working. After that, I asked him if he remembered the weird long object that I pulled out of his knee when we were little children. He said, "yeah!" But, his memory was a little different. He thought that we were in my room when it happened but I remembered being outside in the backyard by the garage. We could have been outside and then came into the house for all I know. The main thing was, he did remember the long weird object. He said, "it seemed like it was an iron wire that shouldn't have been able to fit in my leg, how did that thing even fit?" I don't know how that thing fitted in his whole leg but it actually did happen.

When I retrieved the object from my brother's leg, I was only seven and my brother was just six. At those ages, all we knew about was candy, cartoons, and toys. Implants or abduction never seemed to enter our little minds. Neither did the fact that the weird long object could have possibly been a tracking device of some kind. Maybe it could have even held all the knowledge and power of the universe. Who knows? We didn't know what the heck it was. So, I just threw it on the ground as if it was garbage. Now, I realize that thing was worth more than what anyone on the planet could ever pay. One thing I regret is that we didn't tell our parents about it back in 1984.

Memory 14 - Conversation With Mom

When I finally spoke with my mother, I explained the details about the clock in dad's car and about the object that I pulled out of my brother's knee back in 1984. When I described what the weird long object looked like, mom was definitely intrigued. She said, "Why didn't you tell me sooner?" I couldn't answer that question. I didn't know why I didn't tell her. It was as if I just forgot all about it.

The conversation that we were having must have caused my mom to start thinking about what happened to her because she started touching her neck and telling me about the scar on it. She told me that she started noticing that she had a mark on her neck about two weeks after we got home from our 1984 vacation. Mom said that the scar started off as an irritated bruise and eventually it turned into a noticeable dent in her neck. She said that it used to hurt a lot and give her sharp pains. I looked at her neck and I saw that it did look like it had been cut before but now it was just an old scar. Her scar was located on her neck right where a man's Adam's apple would be. She also said that my dad had a scar on his neck too but he was always reluctant to speak about it.

Mom also spoke to me about the ball of fire and UFO that her and dad saw in 1984. She recalled how afraid dad was to see a ball of fire in the sky because he thought that it would fall and blow us all up. Mom said that she somehow knew the ball of fire wouldn't fall on us. From its speed and trajectory, she thought it might be guided.

After the ball of fire left, mom recalled that the Mother Wheel appeared. She said "they" spoke to her mind telepathically. She said that “they” answered her questions and told her that “they” are our Brothers from The Coalition for Universal Peace. Mom also said that “they” told her that something was going to happen to the planet and “they” were going to help some of the people. Although it seems strange, that's what “they” told mom. My mother said that she had been telling her family members that this is what “they” told her ever since 1984 and I believe her.

After our conversation, mom suggested that I go over to the house on Marlowe Drive to see if I could find the weird long object. It had been seven years since I had seen it and I figured that it was long gone. That week, I did go to Marlowe Drive to see if it was still there. Unfortunately, I didn’t find it. I suspected that if it was still in the backyard; it was buried somewhere covered under the dirt. I would need some type of equipment to find it.

Memory 15 - Cuts And Sores

After mom and I had our discussion, I went to take a bath. While I was in the tub, my mom's neck scar and my brother's knee scar was on my mind. I started looking at my body to see if I had any weird scars that I didn't remember. To my surprise, I actually did. It was a long scar down my whole right forearm. I said to myself, "I don't remember that ever happening. Trust me, I'd remember a long 10 inch scar if it ever happened." The scar looked like it was cut with a precision laser and it had a dot where it started and a dot where it ended. I could not figure out how that scar got on my arm. I wondered why I never even noticed it before. It just didn't make clear sense to me. Then I suddenly thought about the clock in the car. The way it just popped on didn't make any sense either.

A lot of thoughts went through my mind. I thought about how my whole immediate family had weird cuts and sores on our bodies that we couldn't explain. Mom and dad both had scars on their necks but dad never wanted to talk about his scar. Now, I saw that I had a scar down my whole forearm. I said to myself, "Is this real?" My brother had a scar on his knee and I kept picking at it until this weird long object came out of his whole leg. I even remembered that my brother Marcus had a burn on the right side of his face when we returned home in 1984. That burn eventually turned into a black blotch. It's now like an imitation birthmark that he wasn't even born with. I began to rationalize what may have happened for sanity sake. I also began to be glad and grateful that I didn't remember anything traumatic like seeing aliens or being abducted. That would have been too much for me to mentally handle. When I got out of the tub, I had plenty of questions and not one single answer about what actually happened to us.

BEING ON THE PLANET 1
A DIARY OF TRUE EVENTS

Chapter Three

Love, Basketball, and Spaceships

(1995)

Memories 16-20

Memory 16 - I Met The One

I met my life partner on May 12, 1995. It was my eighteenth birthday. I saw Perry in the grocery store while I was buying some potatoes. I noticed that he was very handsome but something about his demeanor made me get off the aisle where he was. He did look like he was up to something devious. Then he came to the next aisle where I was shopping. He was so cute, I completely forgot all about my first impression of him back on aisle one. Then he walked up to me and asked if it was my birthday. I guess it was obvious because I had money pinned on my shirt. With no delay, I told him, "It is my birthday!" Then he asked for my phone number and I gave it to him. Within the hour, he called me on the telephone and I invited him to my birthday party.

That night, Perry attended my party. When he walked up to my cousin's house, I knew that he didn't have a car or much money but I didn't care. The only reason that I felt uncomfortable was because I was wearing a short mini skirt. I explained to him that I was actually a tomboy and I didn't usually wear dresses. I also told him that I was the only girl my parents had and I usually would be with my brothers or boy cousins on a regular day. I let Perry know that I was the kind of female who threw ninja stars, played with bee bee guns, practiced karate, boxing, wrestling, flipping, popping wheelies, climbing trees, walking on handstands, and of course; I played basketball! Basketball was in my genes. My mother and father both could play so it was a natural thing for me to be able to do it too. I told Perry that my brothers and I would play basketball from sun up until it got too dark to see the ball. We could play basketball in the dark. I talked so much about basketball until Perry wanted to see my skills. So, I showed him. I got the ball and I started dribbling it through my legs in that really short mini skirt. Then I passed it to him and said, "check up". He looked impressed.

Perry said, “Girl, I play basketball too, I love it!" He informed me that he was a very good basketball player and we talked about one day going to the basketball court so that we could play each other in a game. Then we started talking about all of the good classic professional ball players such as Michael Jordan and Larry Bird.

We didn’t only talk about basketball though, we also talked about UFOs. Perry found out that night that my family talked about UFOs like it was normal conversation. I told him about what happened to my family back in 1984. He was very interested and he even said that he wished that he could see a UFO.

After our UFO talk, we stayed up all night in my cousin's attic laughing, telling stories, and jokes. We recorded ourselves on a tape recorder. I wish I still had that tape.

Memory 17 - The Hustle Game

Perry and I were together everyday after we met. We became best friends and lovers who played basketball together. One day, after a personal one on one match, I said, "We should use our skills to put money in our pockets. We're going to spend the whole day at the basketball court anyway so why not get paid?" Perry agreed that it was a great idea. So we started going to different courts and asking players to play us for cash. Fortunately, for us; most guys thought that they could beat us so they would put their money up.

Perry and I both had some basketball tricks that were very confusing to most competitors. Although he was only 5'9" and I was 5'11", we'd out-smart the guys who were more physically dominant over us every time. Our opponents never suspected that while playing, we'd just keep winning with our trick moves, amazing jump shots, and endurance. But, we kept winning because Perry could shoot that ball and he would hit three point shots all day long nonstop. He would also give me amazing passes and it just made the other team look bad when I made the shot right in some guy's face.

When we played for money, I tried my best to stay humble and not talk too much. Plenty of times, I wanted to talk junk to our opponents for underestimating us. I kept quiet though because I've seen guys get so pissed off because they lost. Especially because they've lost to a girl and her boyfriend. One time, some dude pushed me down because of his anger and pride. Perry just reached his hand out, helped me up, and said, "Baby lets get dis money!" As teammates, we won every game throughout the summer of 1995. Unfortunately, playing street ball didn't provide us with enough money.

Memory 18 - The Financial Struggle

When I met Perry, he worked at a Cracker Barrel restaurant and I was unemployed. Although we played basketball for a little money on the side, Perry kept encouraging me to get a real job. One day in July of 1995, we went into a Dawn Donuts shop to get donuts and he asked the manager if he could have a job there. The manager immediately hired him. Then he told the manager that he actually had another job but would she consider hiring his girlfriend instead of him. The manager looked at me and said, "She's hired!" I started working as a cashier that day. Within two weeks, Perry worked there too. He was a dishwasher. Unfortunately, it started being a conflict between us because I would get tips from men who flirted with me and Perry would get really jealous. The manager just fired us both because of the drama between us. She said that we argue too much on the job.

After knowing each other for about four months; in August of 1995, Perry and I scraped up enough cash and moved into our first apartment together. We moved into a rough neighborhood on Caldwell Street. It was all that we could afford and it was frustrating. I cried the first night that we stayed in our apartment because we lived above crackheads. They were on the first floor and they only partied and smoked crack all day.

Our apartment didn't have a bedroom, only a living room, kitchen, and bathroom. The bathroom had this old 1920s looking tub with a thick tub stopper and plenty of cabinets. The kitchen had this old 1970s carpet, but we kept it clean and we had plenty of food; thanks to food stamps. All we had in the living room was a pull out bed, a TV, a radio, a video game, and a clock. Some days when we were thankful, we would sit together in silence and listen to the refrigerator hum.

When we listened to music, Perry would always play the song, *Just As Long As We Have Love* by the Spinners. That song would make me cry as I compared it to our financial situation. He would also ask me to play him in the video game all day long. Part of being a tomboy is that we are great at sports. I would win almost every time when we played football, basketball, and boxing. Perry would get mad and throw the video game controller and then say, "Play me again Jaclyn!" It was an everyday festivity and I was honored to beat him all day long.

Memory 19 - The Spaceship Encounter

In September of 1995, Perry asked me if I wanted to go get some pizza. I said, " yeah let me get my jacket." Oddly, before we could leave out of the door of our apartment; I got extremely tired. It was so weird because I wasn't even tired until I touched the door. I told Perry that I had to rest for a minute and then I instantly fell asleep. As I was sleeping, I dreamed that he and I were in the sky and two spaceships crossed right in front of us. In the dream, I tried to see what was behind us but I couldn't. Then I woke up. I looked at the clock and only one minute had passed. Perry asked me if I was ok. I told him that I just dreamed that we both were in the sky and two spaceships crossed. One ship had a red light above it and the other had a blue light. He said, "for-real" then he handed me my jacket and we left out of the door.

We walked over to Perry's mom's house. She lived on Patterson Street, only a couple of blocks away from where we lived on Caldwell. When we arrived, Perry used his mother's phone and he ordered the pizza. We both went outside and sat on the porch while we waited for the pizza delivery man to arrive. As we were sitting on the porch smoking a cigarette, we started talking. While I was speaking to him, I looked up and I noticed two lights blinking in the night sky. They were the size of two regular planes. The two lights were moving towards each other. I said to Perry, "hey, isn't it illegal for planes to cross each other in the sky?" Then I said, "If those lights cross each other, that's going to be similar to what I just dreamed!"

The both of us waited and watched. The blinking lights were moving slowly towards each other but before we could see the two lights cross, another phenomenon occurred which took our attention. We heard a loud sound happening right behind us. It sounded like a loud waterfall or something. As we both turned around to see what the loud sound was, it was a humongous UFO. It appeared above his mom's house from the backyard and it was coming in our direction towards the porch. It was loud when it appeared but in a split second it was totally silent. The UFO was cigar shaped and it looked like a lit up arena floating above the street. It was metallic and it glowed very bright but it didn't have any lights on it at all. It was just lit up from the inside of it's metallic shell. Compared to a plane in the sky, it was about 2,000 times bigger than a regular plane. It was so humongous, my eyes couldn't measure if it was actually here on earth or out in space.

Perry and I watched as the UFO floated south east across his mother's street. Then Perry started hollering saying, "you're psychic Jaclyn, you're psychic" but I didn't say a word. I was just too surprised. Although I wasn't saying anything, Perry was so loud with excitement. He was amped up from what we just saw and how it all happened. He really had been wanting to see a UFO and he got what he wanted. I just stood wondering what was the whole purpose of dreaming about the UFO before it actually happened.

Once the UFO passed over the corner of Martin Luther King Avenue and Patterson Street, we ran to the next street over but the UFO was gone. I stood at the corner of the street wondering how something that big could just disappear so fast. The whole experience happened within seconds. If we were not looking up, we would've missed it. I was bewildered and I felt so small and insignificant. I felt like I didn't know anything about what's really going on in the universe at all. Although we did see a huge UFO, I didn't see any aliens that's for sure. I didn't have any answers about why my family seemed to see UFOs either. I was just left with more questions.

After we walked back to Perry's mother's house, the pizza delivery arrived. We told the pizza man that we just saw a gigantic UFO and we asked him if he saw it too. He just looked at us like we were crazy. He hurried and then sped away suddenly in his car.

Memory 20 - Unexpected Family Obligation

A week after Perry and I saw the huge UFO, we went to the hospital because I felt sick. The doctor came into the room and said, “you're pregnant!" I was shocked but Perry was so happy. He was saying, "yeah, I’m about to have a son!" I wasn't too happy about it though. I had other plans with my life that I hadn't fulfilled yet. Although I did like him, I had only known him for about five months and it seemed too soon for us to have a family. I wasn't happy about our financial situation either. Eventually, I accepted the fact that we were about to have a child. I didn’t know it at the time but the babies would keep coming. I would spend the next seven years having unexpected pregnancies and giving birth to our children. We would have a total of four children together.

BEING ON THE PLANET

1 A DIARY OF TRUE EVENTS

Chapter Four

From Mothership to Motherhood

(1996-2003)

Memories 21-25

Memory 21 - Child Number One

Having our first child destroyed my beautiful model figure. During the pregnancy, I had gained over a hundred pounds by my last trimester. Perry and I went to a dietitian to see how we could slow up the weight gain but I was still gaining five pounds a week. When the baby was born, I couldn't believe that he was only seven pounds, nine ounces.

My mother, my best friend, and Perry were all in the delivery room with me. Perry did leave for a while but then he returned with a completely shaven beard. I had never seen him with his beard shaved before and he looked weird like Barney Rubble from the Flintstones. He told me that he wanted to kiss the baby and that he didn't want to scratch him with his beard. I thought that idea was the sweetest thing in the world. My best friend (Simonne) had her video recorder out and as soon as she saw my private area, she started giggling. She was the most beautiful and animated camera woman ever. My mom was looking like a proud grandparent rocking in a rocking chair by the window. Every time I looked at her, she just smiled. Unfortunately, the baby wasn't positioned correctly and he was in distress. The doctors had to flip him over inside of my stomach. They put some type of clip on his head too so that they could monitor him.

When I pushed the baby out, the nurse laid him under the warm light and Perry said, "hey man" and the baby just smiled. Then Perry asked, "What's wrong with his head?" My mom said, "He just came out of the womb." Perry and I looked at each other and we both seemed to be concerned.

About an hour later, the nurse brought the baby back to our room and he looked very different. His head had gotten circular. He had this superman swirl in the middle of his forehead and a dimple on one side of his face. He was adorable! I checked his whole body to see if anything was wrong. Then I noticed that he had something inside of his little leg. I gently pressed down on it and I never noticed it again. Perry Jr. was born in 1996.

Memory 22 - Child Number Two

Our second child was almost about to be born at church. While the preacher was doing his sermon, I started having vicious contractions. The pastor must have noticed that I was about to have my baby because while he was preaching, he said, "Somebody better take her to the hospital right now!" I wanted to wait until church service was over but the pastor told my cousin (Brigitte) to take me immediately. It's a good thing that we did leave because within twenty minutes after arriving at the hospital, the baby was born.

When the nurse laid her on my stomach, she was all chalky and gooky. She lifted her head straight up and she looked at me as if she was thinking "are you my mother?" I was scared of how intelligent she was. Also, she had some major lungs on her. She cried so loud, it was like she demanded to know who I was and where in the world was she at. When they wiped all of the goo off of her little body, she looked like a white baby. Perry walked in the delivery room while the baby was sleeping. He said, "Why is she so white?" Then he looked at me as if I cheated on him. I said, "Apparently because of our mother’s light skin."

When I was being discharged from the hospital, the doctors came into the room and told us that they found something wrong with our baby’s hip. I was frantic when they said that they may need to break her hip. When they discharged me, I left the hospital crying because I had to leave without my baby. While we were driving away, I heard the song, *All My Life* by K-Ci and JoJo on the radio. It was the first time that I heard that song. It made me cry even more. It became my theme song for my baby girl. The next day, the hospital called me to come get her. They decided that the procedure wasn't necessary. Our daughter Paris was born in 1997.

Memory 23 - Ectopic Pregnancy

On my third pregnancy, I sat at the table and had a really deep talk with God. The conversation was about how I was young and had two children already and how now I was pregnant again. At the time, our son was two and our daughter was six months old. I explained to God that I didn't want to have another child at that time. My exact words were; "lord I don't want to have an abortion but I'm struggling. I already have two children and it's been too hard to provide for them. Whatever your will is, I will do but I don't want to have another child right now. If there is anything that you can do to help me please do it. Amen." Immediately after my prayer, it felt like something broke inside of me. I told Perry that I needed to go to the hospital but he didn't believe anything was wrong with me. I told him that it didn't matter to me if he believed me or not; I was in pain and I had to get to the hospital immediately.

When I arrived at the hospital, the doctor examined me and explained that I had an ectopic pregnancy. He said that I had internal bleeding and that I needed to have an emergency surgery immediately because the fetus could kill me. The doctor also said that after the procedure was done

I wouldn't be able to have any more children. As the nurses consoled me and talked about how young I was and how I wouldn’t be able to have children anymore; I was ignoring everything they were saying. I knew that I had just prayed to God about my situation and I knew that God would work everything out the way he saw fit. Although I feared surgery, I accepted my fate. I went into surgery repeatedly saying over and over again, "Jesus help me lord!" I said those words until the anesthesia put me out. When I awoke, I was in a lot of pain but I felt like my prayer was answered. I was ok with not being able to have a child at that time.

Memory 24 - Child Number Three

Our third child snuck her way into the world. I found out that I was pregnant after having a deep relentless pain in my back. I could hardly walk for about six months. So, I finally went to the emergency room to see what the issue was. The doctor asked me if I was pregnant and I told him that I couldn't have children any more. He gave me a urine pregnancy test and it was negative.

The nurse took me into a room and she used a scope to see what was the reason for my back pain. While she was moving the scope around, she said, “uh oh.” I said, "Oh what is it?" She turned the screen so that I could see. I saw a big baby on the screen sucking its thumb. The next thing I know, there were doctors coming in the room from everywhere. They drew my blood and did calculations on the conception and due date. After they did an ultrasound, the nurse said, “you're six months pregnant.” I was in shock because I was having menstrual periods.

When Perry arrived, I told him, “guess what was wrong with my back? I’m pregnant! As a matter of fact, I’m six months pregnant!” I told him that we have only three months to prepare for this baby. He said, “Stop lying, you can't have children anymore." Then I showed him the ultrasound picture and the hospital papers. He was stuck in his position for a couple of seconds. Then he smiled. Leaving the hospital, the baby kicked for the first time. When she was born, she actually was trying to talk. Our daughter Peru was born in 2001.

Memory 25 - Child Number Four

Our fourth child and I almost died together. One night, I woke up and went to the bathroom. Suddenly, a baby's head came out. I was so scared, I pushed her back in. It was a stupid thing to do but I didn't know what else to do. I didn't want to have her in the bathroom by myself. At that time, I knew that I could get pregnant but I had no morning sickness and I continued to have menstrual periods. Also, I was overweight and it was hard for me to tell if I was pregnant or not.

I wobbled into the room and woke Perry up and he sped me to the hospital at about one hundred miles per hour. When we arrived, the doctors told us that I was at ten centimeters and that I couldn’t have any pain medication. I was in such serious pain. It was the worst pain that I've ever felt in my life. When the doctors told me that I could push, the baby came right out but she wasn't breathing. The umbilical cord was wrapped around her neck and she was looking blue. I watched horrified as the doctor removed the cord from her neck. Then the doctor hit her on her little feet and she started crying. I was so relieved! I was so happy, I started clapping!

Frantically, the doctor pushed me back and he asked me if I wanted to die. I said, "Die...No I don't want to die!" I was so excited because my baby was alive, I didn't notice that I was hemorrhaging all over the floor. I looked down and saw blood pouring like a running faucet. Then Perry said, "hey what's wrong with her?" He and the doctor looked so afraid. Then the nurses rushed and put me on oxygen. After that, I started feeling a little dizzy. At that very moment, I was thinking, " oh lord I don't have time to die!" Quickly, the doctor stuffed both of his hands into my private area to try to stop the bleeding. Without any pain medication it was traumatic. I was about to bleed out but the doctor did some sort of procedure and he saved my life. The placenta detached wrongly. Our daughter Porsche was born in 2003.

BEING ON THE PLANET 1

A DIARY OF TRUE EVENTS

Chapter Five

Multiple Sightings

Memories 26-29

Memory 26 - The Concerned UFO

[redacted]

On the fourth of July 2007, Perry and I took our four children downtown to see the Flint Fireworks. We were mad at each other that night but we tried to act happy so that our children could have some fun. When we made it downtown, some of our family members were parked waiting for us at the Rally's Restaurant. We got out of the car and greeted them. After we all hugged each other, all of us grownups poured our drinks and got our tailgate party started.

The children were dancing while I vibed to the loud music that someone was playing. Then I climbed on the top of the car and watched as my children were going from car to car to socialize with their cousins. Unfortunately, Perry started getting drunk. He was so loud and it was irritating and embarrassing. I was having a nice time with my children though.

After the firework display was over, everyone agreed to go watch more fireworks on the other side of Flint. When we left, we all followed each other in our cars to this abandoned school. It was where the local drug dealers provided a spectacular firework show. They did it all night long and they did it every year. When we drove in the parking lot, it was full of smoke and it looked like a war zone with fireworks going off everywhere. It was so exciting but scary at the same time. Although it was thrilling, it was dangerous. When a firework hit the window of the car, we all decided that it was time to go.

It was about 12 am when we arrived home so we sent the children into the house for bed. Perry and I continued to sit outside in the car. I knew that we were about to argue and I didn't want our children to hear it. Our argument was about financial issues and infidelity. At the time, I had just bought our first home and even though I was working hard at General Motors, the mortgage was taking a toll on me. Perry was unemployed and he seemed to be cheating. He denied cheating but my intuition wouldn't allow me to believe him.

I was very hurt and furiously angry at Perry. We both were cursing and hollering non stop. I yelled and cried so much until my throat was hoarse. While we argued, I kept looking through the front window of the car. Straight up the driveway, I noticed this odd bright light in the night sky. It was directly in my range of view. It had been there ever since we arrived home. I would periodically look up and see it but I didn't say anything about it.

After a couple of hours of sitting in the car arguing, I brought to Perry's attention that there was this big bright light in the sky. He looked up and with a funky attitude, he told me that he noticed it too. Then we continued to argue. That night, we argued for about a total of four hours all together. Around 4am in the morning, we both were just about worn out. Suddenly, the bright light just bolted straight towards us and it flew over the car and it did a u- turn above our street. Perry and I both jumped out of the car quickly and watched the bright light speed through the sky. It took off so fast as if it was some kind of rocket. It looked like something from a Sci-Fi movie. After it did a U-turn, it went straight down our street going north until it was out of sight. Then Perry said, "what the f..." and I said, "I knew that wasn't just a star". After seeing that; we didn't argue anymore. We both just went into the house.

While we were standing in the doorway of our home, Perry told me that he was sorry for hurting me. At that point, I was so tired until I just shook my head and headed to the bedroom to get some sleep. I wondered what that bright light was though. It just sat there for so many hours as if it was a giant bright star in the night sky but it was only imitating a star. I call it the concerned UFO because it did just sit there throughout our whole argument and then left when we stopped arguing.

Memory 27 - The Northside UFO

On a summer day in 2011, Perry and I had just dropped the children off and we were headed over to my mom's house. While we drove there, I noticed how beautiful the sky was. The sun was almost about to set and the sky looked very orangish with red streaks. We were coming from the Beecher district and it was very bright and blinding as we drove up Martin Luther King Avenue. Then we made a right turn on Pierson Road. After we turned, we saw a metallic UFO hovering in the sky.

I couldn’t tell how big the UFO was but I did see that it was swaying slowly from left to right. I don’t know how far away it was but as we continued to drive towards Clio Road, the size of it never changed. It was as if the closer we got to it, the farther away it really was. When we made a left turn on Fleming Road, we were looking out of the right-side windows watching the UFO. That's when we could see it hovering and swaying between the trees. As we continued down Fleming Road, we just watched it hover from side to side. Once we got to Pasadena Street, we had to stop driving because of traffic. There were cars everywhere! People were stopping and looking up out of their windows. Everyone wondered what that thing was. I even saw a police officer in his police car looking up at the UFO in the sky. After we got through the traffic, we headed towards my mom's house and when we got there, I hurried out of the car and told her and her husband (Brian) what we just saw.

While I was talking to my mom and her husband about the UFO, my cousin (Camille) called me on the phone. Around that time, it was night. Camille said, "We just saw a UFO on Welch Boulevard!" I said to Camille, "we just saw it too!" I explained to her that we were only a couple of blocks away and the whole northside of Flint possibly saw that UFO. She said that from her range of view, the UFO was diamond shaped and that it came towards her car. Then she said, "It hovered above the trees". I told her, from my range of view; I couldn't tell the shape of it but we saw it hovering between the trees as well. It definitely was an amazing sight to see. I call it the Northside UFO because it flew in daylight on the Northside of Flint, Michigan. That happened just three years before the Flint Water Crisis began.

Memory 28 - Two Suns In The Sky

[redacted]

In January of 2012, around 5pm I was driving my children around in my minivan. We were headed to a family gathering. While driving, I stopped at the red light and I noticed that there were two suns in the sky. I told the children, "look up, there's two suns!" They really couldn't see them from the back seat of the van. So I hurried and pulled the van over to a side street. I told the children to get out of the van so that they could look up at the sky. All four of my children were so amazed. As we all looked to the right side of the sky, there was the sun and as we looked to the left; there was also a Sun. The sun on the right side of the sky looked like it burned hotter and it had a blue flare around it. The Sun to the left looked like it regularly does. I know that there is only one sun in our solar system but that day it was actually two. I don't know what that was in the sky but it definitely was a massive sphere. It looked like a gigantic ball of fire.

BEING ON THE PLANET 1
A DIARY OF TRUE EVENTS

Chapter Six

Talking To Mom About The Mother Wheel

Talking To Mom About The Mother Wheel

While writing this book, my mother and I had a really deep conversation about the connection between UFOs, the balls of fire in the sky, and the true children of Israel (Us). Mom said, "We Black descendants of enslaved people here in the wilderness of North America are the true children of Israel." We talked about how black people were the only people in bondage for 400 years and now we suffer oppression in the Mystery Babylon described in the bible. According to the Bible, the chosen people of God (The real children of Israel) are oppressed by Pharaoh and guided by a pillar of fire by night and a cloud by day. As we conversed, mom reminded me that prior to the appearance of the Mother Wheel in 1984, a ball of fire followed us in the sky.

Mom stated that it was not a coincidence that the ball of fire followed us before she saw the Great Mother Wheel in the sky. She believes that the experience is connected to our ancestors, the oppression that we have experienced as Black people, and the U.S. governments assassination of her brother Mark Clark, a Black Panther Party Leader. In 1969, he was assassinated by the U.S. government and FBI COINTELPRO. The year prior to the Mother Wheel experience, mom learned that the agents responsible for her brother's death received immunity. No one was brought to justice.

Mom shared with me how in the book of Ezekiel the wheels were envisioned in the year 995 B.C. During that time, Ezekiel was in a captivity in Babylon. She said, "That was prophetic. Now, we are in the Mystery Babylon (America) and Ezekiel's wheel is a reality!" She also said, "With the coming of Allah, who came in the person of Master Fard Muhammad, signals the rise of the Black people and end of this present world." My mother is a member of the Nation of Islam and she believes in the Nation whole heartedly.

According to the Nation of Islam, the angels are in the wheels that travel in the sky. My mom believes that the real angels are the original Asiatic Black Man. She says that they are people like us but with extraordinary powers and the ability to travel on the wheels. She doesn't believe that "they" are little grey men with big heads and slanted black eyes. She thinks that type of "alien" is only government propaganda.

Mom bears witness that the Great Mother Wheel is a half mile by a half mile in size. Mom said,"according to the Nation of Islam the Great Mother Wheel and its 1,500 baby wheels are commanded by Allah, Master Fard Muhammad, and The Most Honorable Elijah Muhammad the Exalted Christ." Mom also said that the Honorable Minister Louis Farrakhan, (National Representative for The Most Honorable Elijah Muhammad) visited the Mother Wheel during a more than a vision-like experience on September 17th 1985. During his experience, he spoke with the Most Honorable Elijah Muhammad.

When we talked about so-called UFOs, mom said, "The wheels have two functions, the destruction of Satan's world and the establishment of a new world." Lastly, mom said that if anyone is skeptical about her experience they should engage in further research and examination.

Chapter Seven

Why I Believe in UFOs

Why I Believe In UFO's

In this book, I explained my UFO encounters and other phenomena that happened to my family. My first UFO encounter occurred when I was seven years old. It was 1984 and my family was on a summer vacation. While we were driving to our destination, my parents said that a gigantic UFO hovered above our car on the highway. My mother said that whatever was in that UFO spoke to her mind telepathically. My dad complained about how the clock in his brand new 1984 Buick LeSabre mysteriously stopped working. Some type of weird anomaly occurred that stopped the clock. My dad told everyone in the car to never tell anyone about the UFO encounter because people would think that we were crazy. So we continued out our 1984 vacation as if the UFO experience never happened.

Sometime during that summer; after we returned home from our vacation, I pulled a weird long object out of my younger brother's knee. The object was about ten to twelve inches long and it had hieroglyphic writing on it. Being a young child, I didn't know what that thing was. So, I threw it on the ground and it seems as if we both instantly forgot all about it. We didn't even tell our parents and I don't know why? At that time, we were too young to really understand the concept of UFO'S, aliens, abduction, or implants.

Seven years later, I was a fourteen year old teenager. It was 1991 and my parents had broken up. We were having major family issues. One day, my dad and I were sitting and talking in his old Buick LeSabre. We were talking about our family issues. Suddenly, the clock in my dad's car mysteriously just clicked back on and it started working again. It was odd because that clock hadn't worked every since our UFO encounter of 1984. When the clock resumed, it immediately sparked a memory in my mind of what happened when I was seven years old. I remembered that after we returned from our vacation in 1984, I pulled this weird black long object out of my brother's knee. The object was about ten to twelve inches long and it had something similar to hieroglyphic writing on it. I don't know why I didn't tell my parents about it back in 1984 but the clock coming back to life definitely caused me to remember it and I finally started telling people about it. I even went searching for the object but by the time I went looking, it was long gone. The last time that I had seen it was in 1984. After I threw it on the ground, I never saw it again. I asked my brother if he remembered it and he did remember it as well. I finally spoke to my mom about how the 1984 encounter affected us and how after it happened; we all had cuts and sores on our bodies that we couldn't explain.

My second UFO encounter happened in 1995. I had just met my children's father (Perry). On the day that I met him, I told him all about what happened to my family back in 1984. He was very interested in my UFO conversation. He even said that he wished that he could see a UFO. About four months after I met him, I dreamed that he and I saw a UFO together. Amazingly, that very same day we both actually witnessed a massive UFO in real life. That was the first time that he thought that I was a psychic because of my dream that came true.

A week after Perry and I saw the huge UFO, I found out that I was pregnant. Soon after that, it seemed as if the babies kept coming. I spent seven years establishing our family. Once we were done having children, Perry and I both witnessed two more UFO sightings together. I've had a total of four UFO encounters throughout my lifetime. I've seen other strange things going on in the sky that looked like balls of fire as well. Ultimately, all of the above is why I am definitely a believer. Now, I refer to those so-called UFOs as IFO's (Identified Flying Objects), Baby Wheels and The Great Mother Wheel!.

BEING ON THE PLANET 1

A DIARY OF TRUE EVENTS

Roll Call, Who's Seen It?

Roll Call, Who's Seen It?

Throughout my lifetime, numerous family members have all told me that they've witnessed strange things going on in the sky. My parents saw a UFO back in 1984. Whatever was in that Mother Wheel spoke to my mom. My grandmother on my Clark side of the family said that she saw a UFO but she didn't like to talk about it. My aunt Felisa said that she saw a UFO while driving on the highway. My cousin Cassanova said that he saw a UFO in the Flint projects. My cousin April said that she saw a UFO in Flint near Northern High School. My uncle Charles said that he saw a UFO in the Howard Estate Projects in Flint. My uncle Robert said that he saw a UFO in Peoria, Illinois and Flint, Michigan. I have plenty of other cousins, aunts, and uncles who all said that they have seen UFOs as well. I believe their testimonies because I have witnessed seeing a UFO more than a couple of times. It was like seeing the power of the universe right before my eyes. It made me a believer!

About the Author

About The Author

Jaclyn (Clark) Hodge

Jaclyn (Clark) Hodge was born in Flint, Michigan on May 12, 1977. She is the first child born to Minister Phil Hodge Sr. and Sister Rose X (Clark) Morris. As a child, Jaclyn was a saxophonist who participated in school marching bands and city orchestras. She also played basketball for various teams. As an older adult, Jaclyn obtained her GED and attended college. She was an all A's student who studied advanced curriculums such as Mathematics and Physics. She majored in Photonics (the study of light energy).

Jaclyn is a poet who loves to perform poetic rhymes. She's also a songwriter that plays the guitar, piano, saxophone, and writes sheet music. Her latest venture is being an editor and author. Jaclyn has created and edited hundreds of commercial videos and two books. She is the editor of the book Chronicle of the Seventh Son Black Panther Mark Clark. Also, she is the author and co-editor of Being On the Planet - A Diary of True Events.

Jaclyn has spent over 25 years with her life partner Perry Alexander. They enjoy playing basketball and video games together. Although they have had some rough times, they stuck with each other. The couple has four children; Perry Jr., Paris, Peru, and Porsche. Their children carry the legacy of being talented, intuitive, intelligent, musically inclined, and gifted with great basketball skills. She is extremely proud and beyond fortunate to be their mother. Of her whole family she proclaims, "The Clark's, Hodge's, and Alexander's are all Kings and Queens." To her family, Jaclyn (Clark) Hodge dedicates her book Being on the Planet – A Diary of True Events.

BEING ON THE PLANET

1 A DIARY OF TRUE EVENTS

UFO Believer - A Poetic-Paragraph

UFO Believer - A Poetic-Paragraph

by Jaclyn(Clark) Hodge

My family had a close encounter of the fifth kind, back in 1984. We were traveling down the highway on 69, driving in a white Buick four door. My mom said, the UFO spoke to her mind. My dad said, "Jesus help us Lord". The clock stopped and we lost time, but we don't remember being on board. Seven years went by, then the clock resumed, it started working again like it was never broken. And in my mind, A memory loomed, I remembered something that was never spoken. I remembered one weird afternoon, from my brother's knee an object was poken. And I noticed in my bathroom, a sore on my arm while I was soaken. I haven't figured it all out yet, maybe that UFO really landed? On our bodies we checked and checked, looked like they cut our flesh and scanned it. My mom and dad had cuts on their necks, I just didn't understand it. The last thing that I'd expect is that my whole family was implanted. Years later, I dreamed I saw a UFO. The next thing I know, I really did. It was my second encounter since eighty foe, I was no longer a little kid. I don't know if the government ever found it, I don't know if it ever showed up on the grid, but through the atmosphere it pounded, it sounded like it did a skid. It had me so astounded, right in the open it wasn’t hid at all. A cigar shape with a weird rounded thing on the top of the lid is what I saw. This was not a UFO on a TV show, not a UFO on a movie neither, As far as aliens goes...I haven’t seen any of those, Hey I'm not Sigourney Weaver. But I’ve seen four different UFOs. It's enough for me to have UFO Fever. What happened to me is very real so, that’s why I'm a UFO Believer!

BEING ON THE PLANET 1

A DIARY OF TRUE EVENTS

Made in the USA
Columbia, SC
17 November 2024

46817272R00065